Oxford Jun Workbook 6A

by Rosemary Carver and Jennifer Brain
illustrated by Phyllida Legg

Name

Oxford Junior Workbook 6A builds on the work of *Oxford Junior Workbook 6*. There are exercises on *ee*, *ea*, and *oo*; *sh* and *ch* are revised and *th* and *wh* added. Time-telling and the interpretation of clock faces are introduced on pp. 10–11, preceded by a preliminary exercise on p. 9. Comparatives and superlatives are introduced on pp. 21–3, together with the idea of comparative distance, both linear (pp. 12–13) and concentric (p. 24). Work on alphabetical order continues on p. 26–7.

Oxford Junior Workbooks

Introductory Books by Jenny Ackland and Jennifer Brain

Introductory	Book A	0 19 838044 5
Introductory	Book B	0 19 838046 1

Main series
by Clifford Carver

1	0 19 834374 4
2	0 19 834375 2
3	0 19 834379 5
4	0 19 834386 8
5	0 19 834392 2
6	0 19 834393 0
7	0 19 834394 9
8	0 19 834395 7

Parallel series
by Stephen Jackson,
Jennifer Brain, and Rosemary Carver

1a	0 19 838009 7
2a	0 19 838010 0
3a	0 19 838011 9
4a	0 19 838012 7
5a	0 19 838036 4
6a	0 19 838037 2
7a	0 19 838038 0
8a	0 19 838039 9

Workbooks by Jenny Ackland

Pre-reading Activity Books

Book 1	0 19 838048 8
Book 2	0 19 838049 6
Book 3	0 19 838050 X
Book 4	0 19 838051 8

Pre-reading Topic Books

Book 1	0 19 838055 0
Book 2	0 19 838056 9
Book 3	0 19 838059 3
Book 4	0 19 838060 7

A First Writing Book
0 19 838053 4

A Second Writing Book
0 19 838054 2

A Third Writing Book
0 19 838061 5

A Fourth Writing Book
0 19 838062 3

Oxford University Press, Walton Street, Oxford OX2 6DP

Oxford New York Toronto
Delhi Bombay Calcutta Madras Karachi
Petaling Jaya Singapore Hong Kong Tokyo
Nairobi Dar es Salaam Cape Town
Melbourne Auckland
and associated companies in
Berlin Ibadan

Oxford is a trade mark of Oxford University Press

© Oxford University Press 1979

School Edition   ISBN 0 19 838037 2
First published 1979
Reprinted 1983, 1984, 1985, 1988, 1989

Trade Edition   ISBN 0 19 838041 0
First published 1979
Reprinted 1989

Printed in Hong Kong

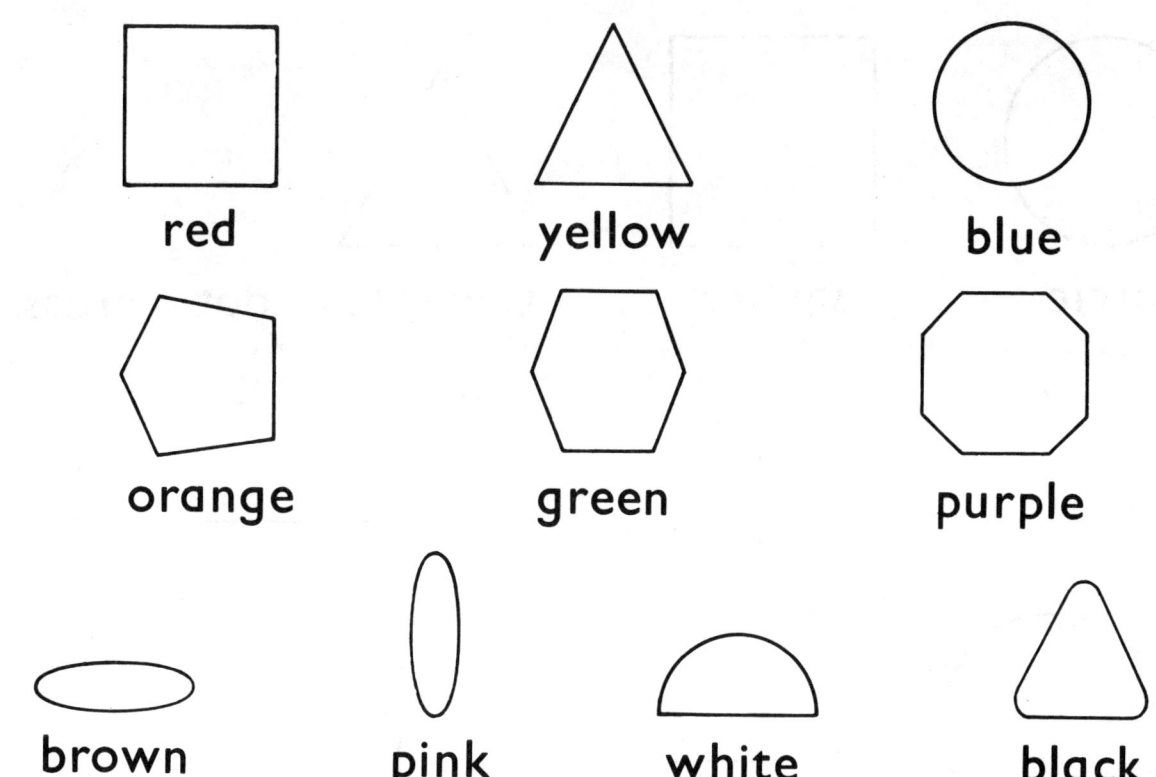

red	yellow	blue		
orange	green	purple		
brown	pink	white	black	

a b c d e f g h i j k l m n o p q r s t u v w x y z

1 one 2 two 3 three 4 four 5 five

6 six 7 seven 8 eight 9 nine 10 ten

11 eleven 12 twelve 13 thirteen 14 fourteen 15 fifteen

16 sixteen 17 seventeen 18 eighteen 19 nineteen 20 twenty

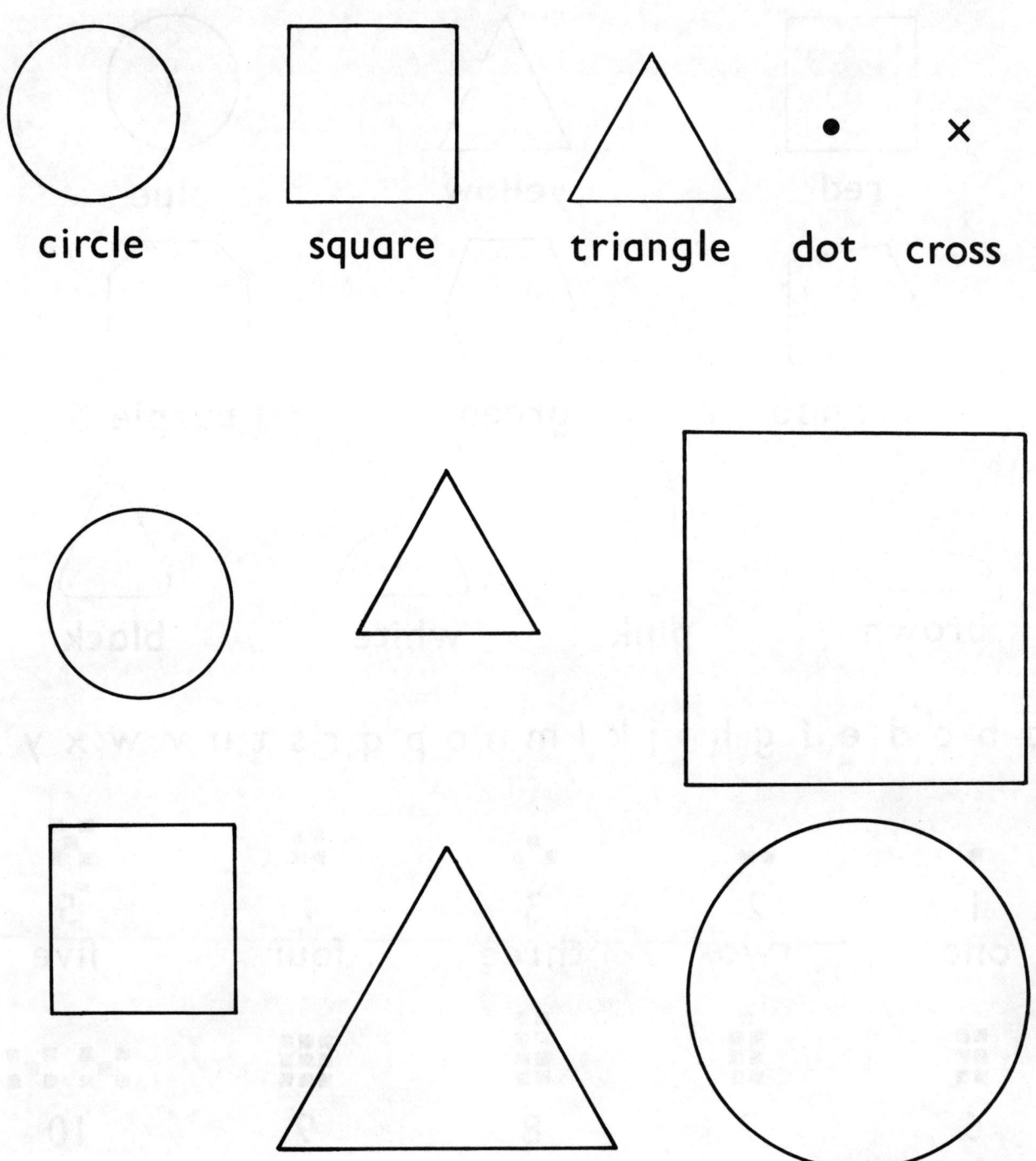

draw five red dots in the little square

draw nine blue crosses in the little circle

draw eight orange dots in the little triangle

draw thirteen purple dots in the big triangle

draw sixteen green crosses in the big square

draw nineteen black crosses in the big circle

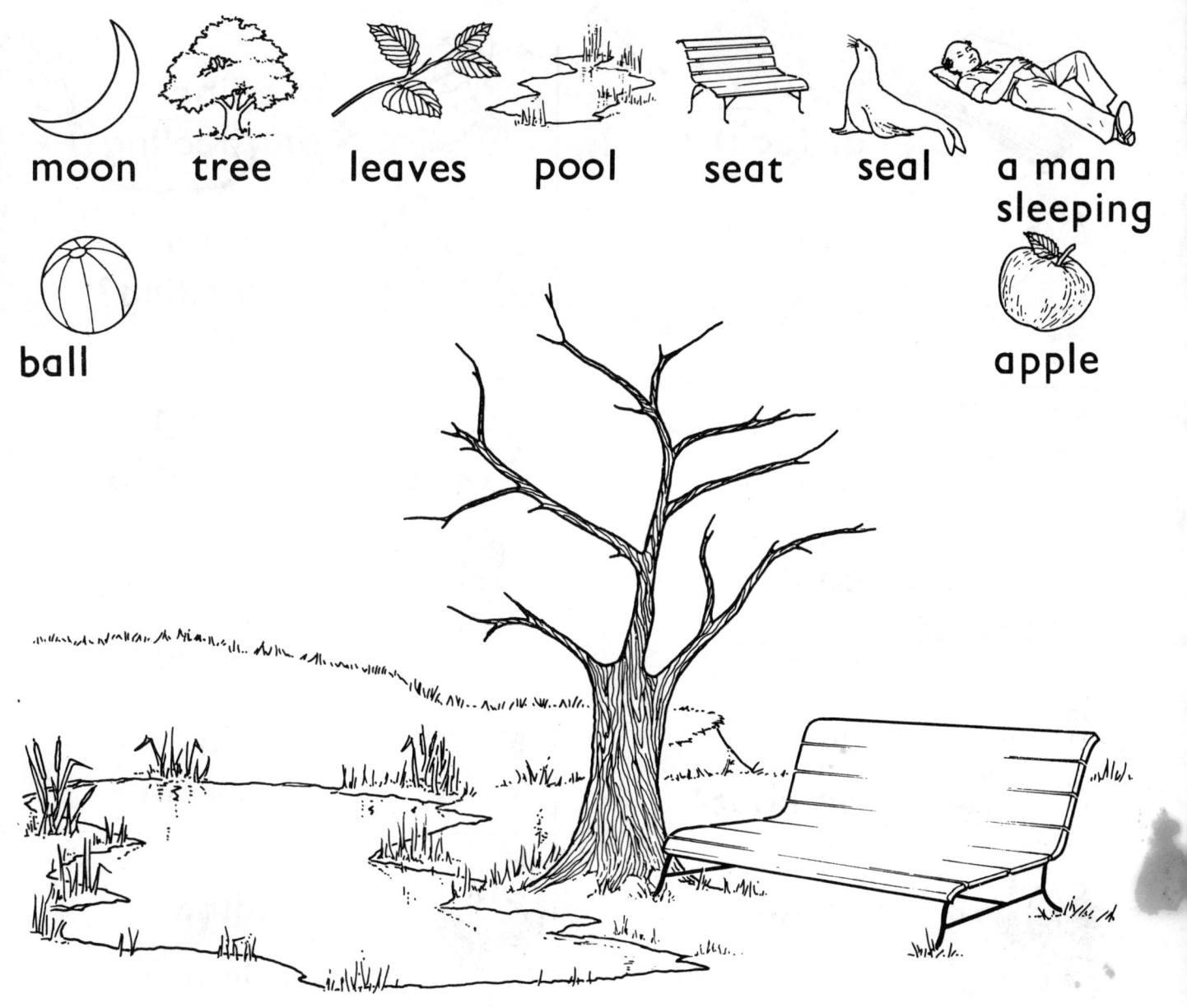

draw three red leaves on the tree

draw four yellow leaves on the tree

draw six brown leaves under the tree

draw two green apples on the tree

draw the moon in the sky

draw a black seal with a red ball in the pool

draw a man sleeping on the seat

draw a red apple falling on the man's head

 boot or (book)?

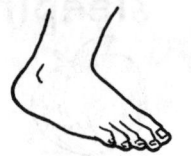 foot or root?

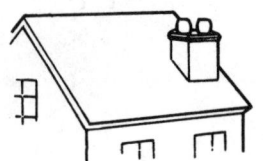 root or roof?

 pool or boot?

 book or boot?

 wool or wood?

 spoon or stool?

 hook or hoof?

 wool or wood?

 mood or moon?

 peeping or (peeling)?

 meeting or feeding?

 creeping or sleeping?

 sleeping or sweeping?

 seeing or seeming?

 reading or leading?

 leaping or leading?

 leading or leaning?

 hearing or heating?

 heating or eating?

ee ee
ea ea

l _ea_ f

tr _ _

s _ _ ing

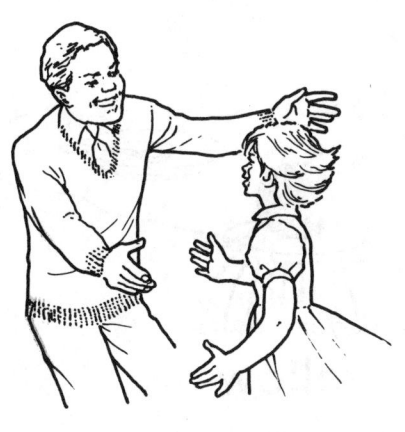
m _ _ ting

_ _ ting

sl _ _ ping

l _ _ ding

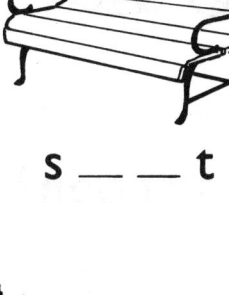
s _ _ t

sw _ _ ping

s _ _ l

is the wool on a yellow stool? yes

is the red boot in a wood?

is the orange woman eating with a spoon?

is the green man seeing a wood?

is the purple man leaping into a pool?

is the orange woman reading a boot?

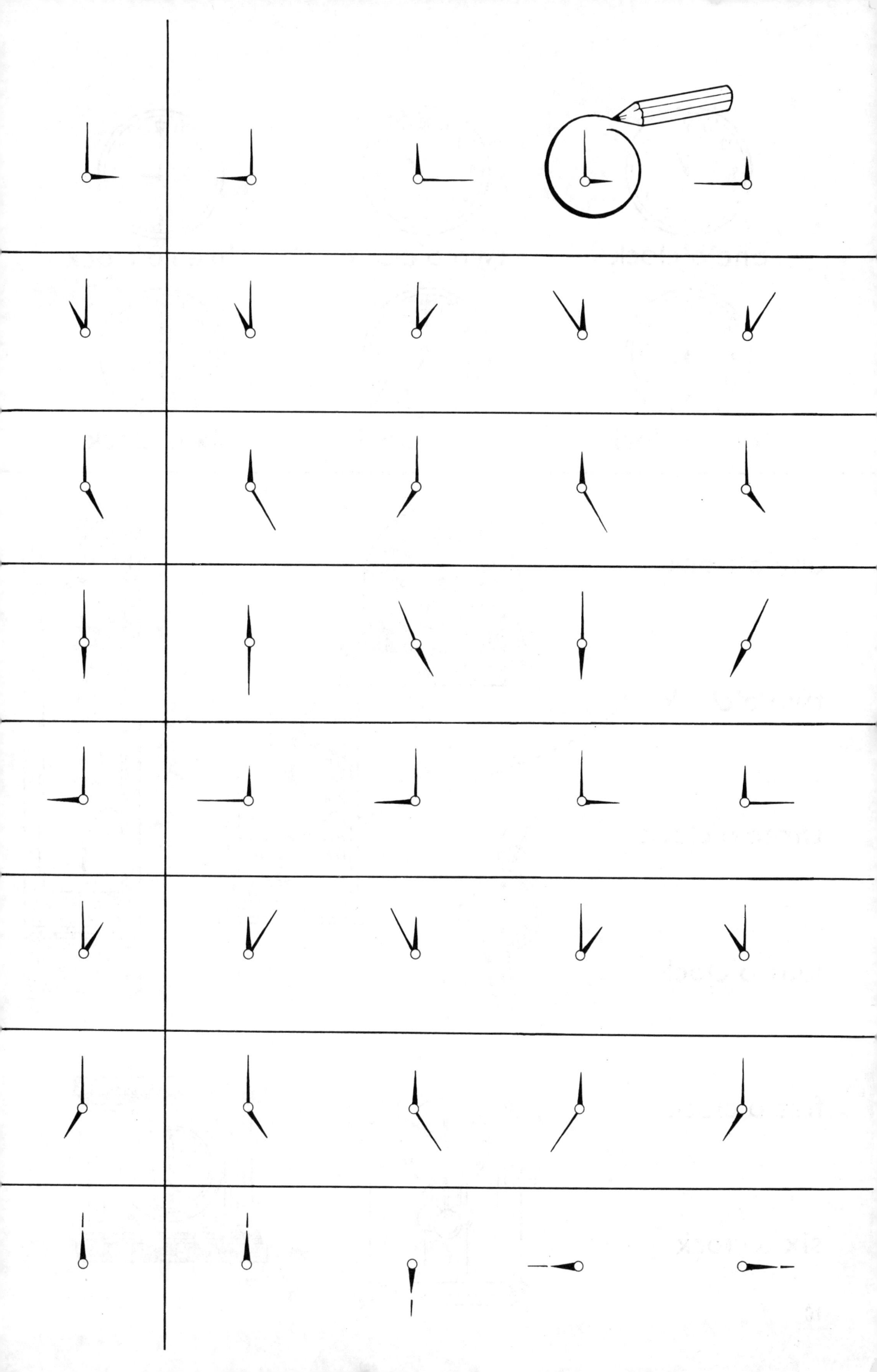

 one o'clock
 two o'clock
 three o'clock
 four o'clock
 five o'clock
 six o'clock

one o'clock

two o'clock

three o'clock

four o'clock

five o'clock

six o'clock

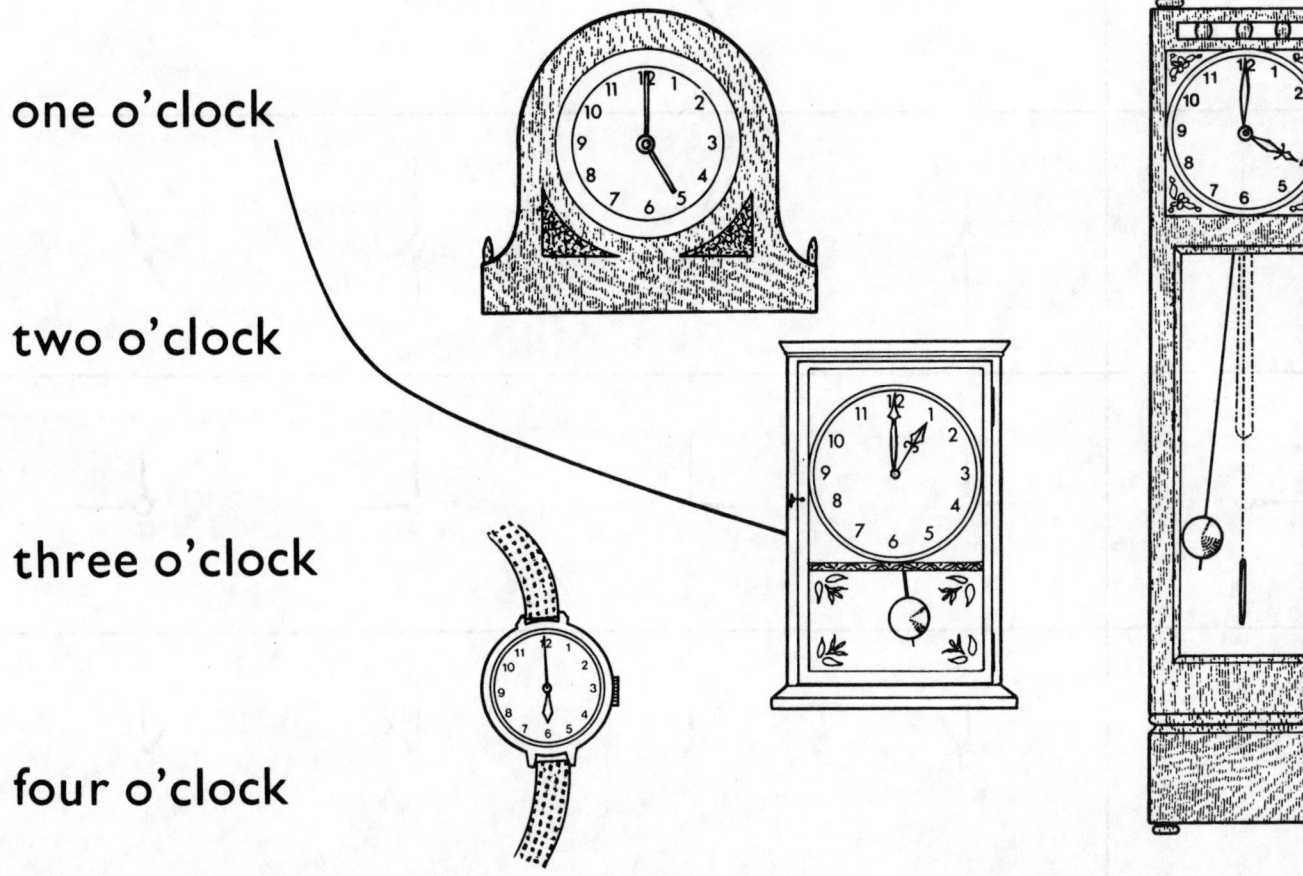
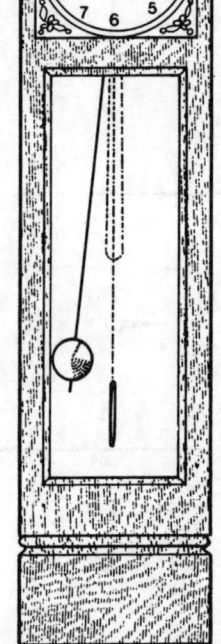
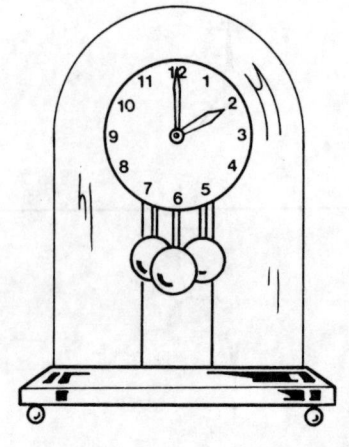

seven o'clock   eight o'clock   nine o'clock

ten o'clock   eleven o'clock   twelve o'clock

---

seven o'clock

eight o'clock

nine o'clock

ten o'clock

eleven o'clock

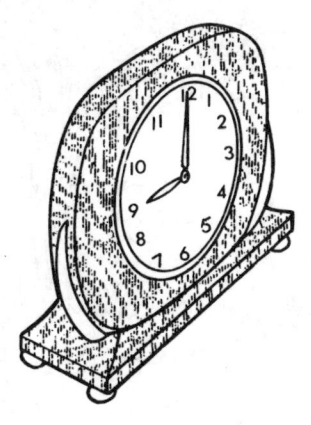

twelve o'clock

colour the picture

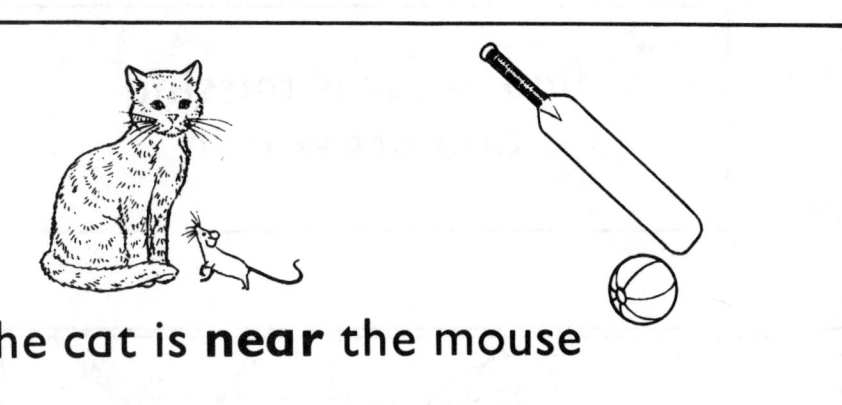

the cat is **near** the mouse

the bat is **near** the ball

the man is near the

| bridge | pool | (house) |

the sheep is near the

| gate | seat | cow |

the birds are near the

| church | tree | car |

the girl is near the

| seat | man | sheep |

the flowers are near the

| boy | house | pool |

the pool is near the

| bridge | church | house |

the dog is near the

| boy | girl | man |

the car is near the

| tree | seat | house |

find what is missing and draw it in

colour the picture

pirate    whale   grey   treasure

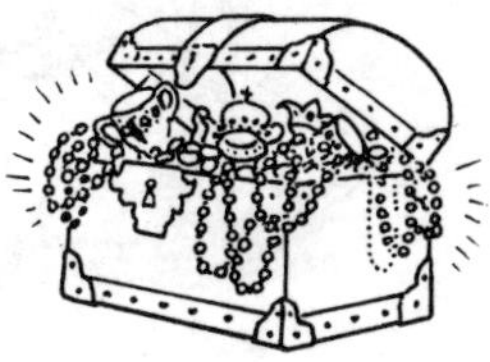

red   orange   green   purple

blue

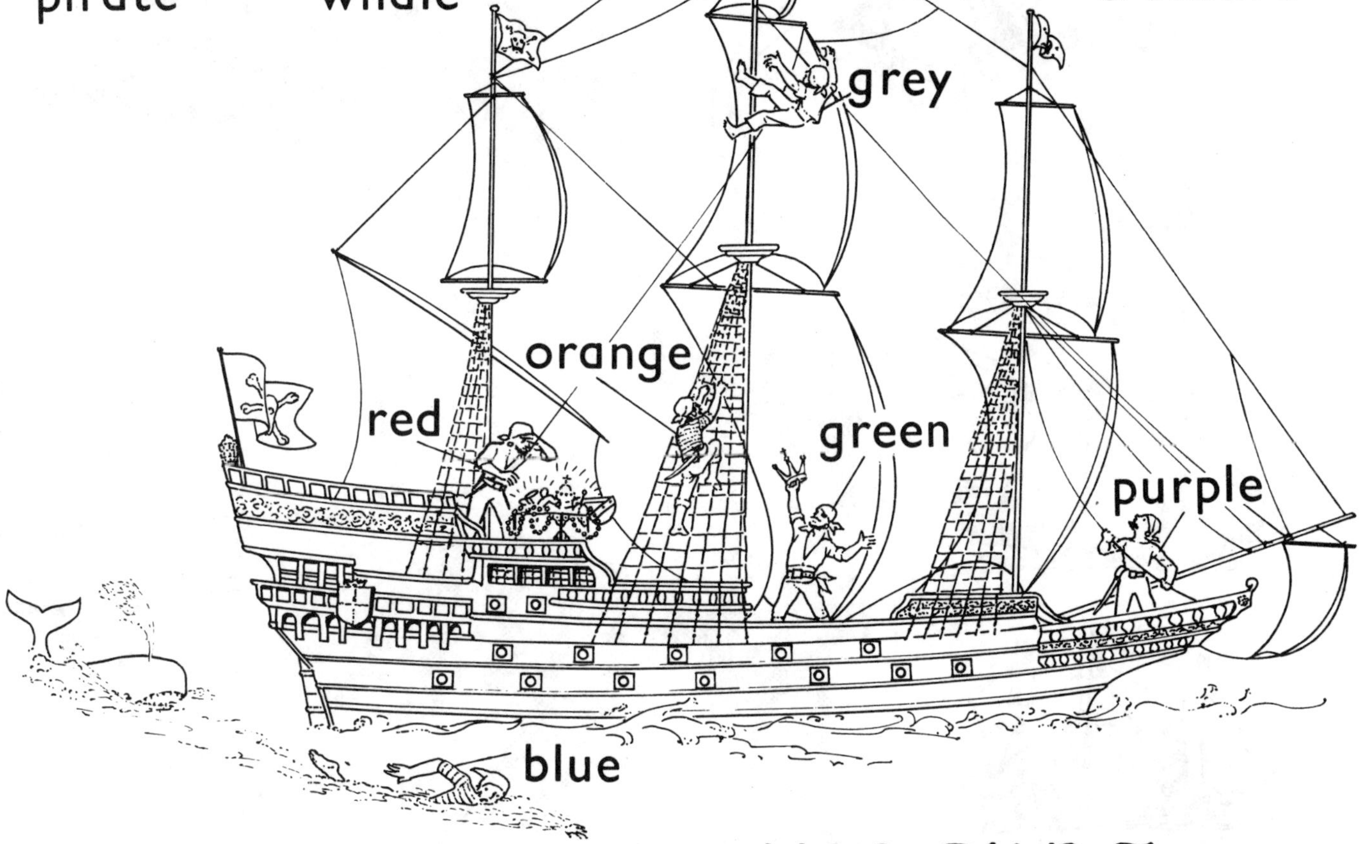

yes or no

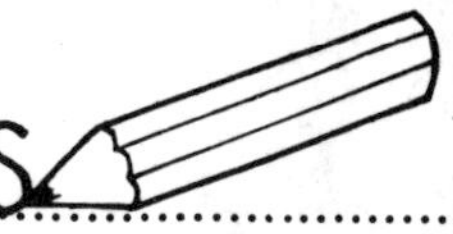

is the orange pirate climbing? yes
is the green pirate swimming? ....
is the grey pirate falling? ....
is the purple pirate looking at the treasure? ....
is the red pirate looking at the treasure? ....
is the blue pirate holding a crown? ....
is the green pirate holding a rope? ....
is the whale chasing the red pirate? ....

 chasing    swimming    climbing    falling    holding    looking

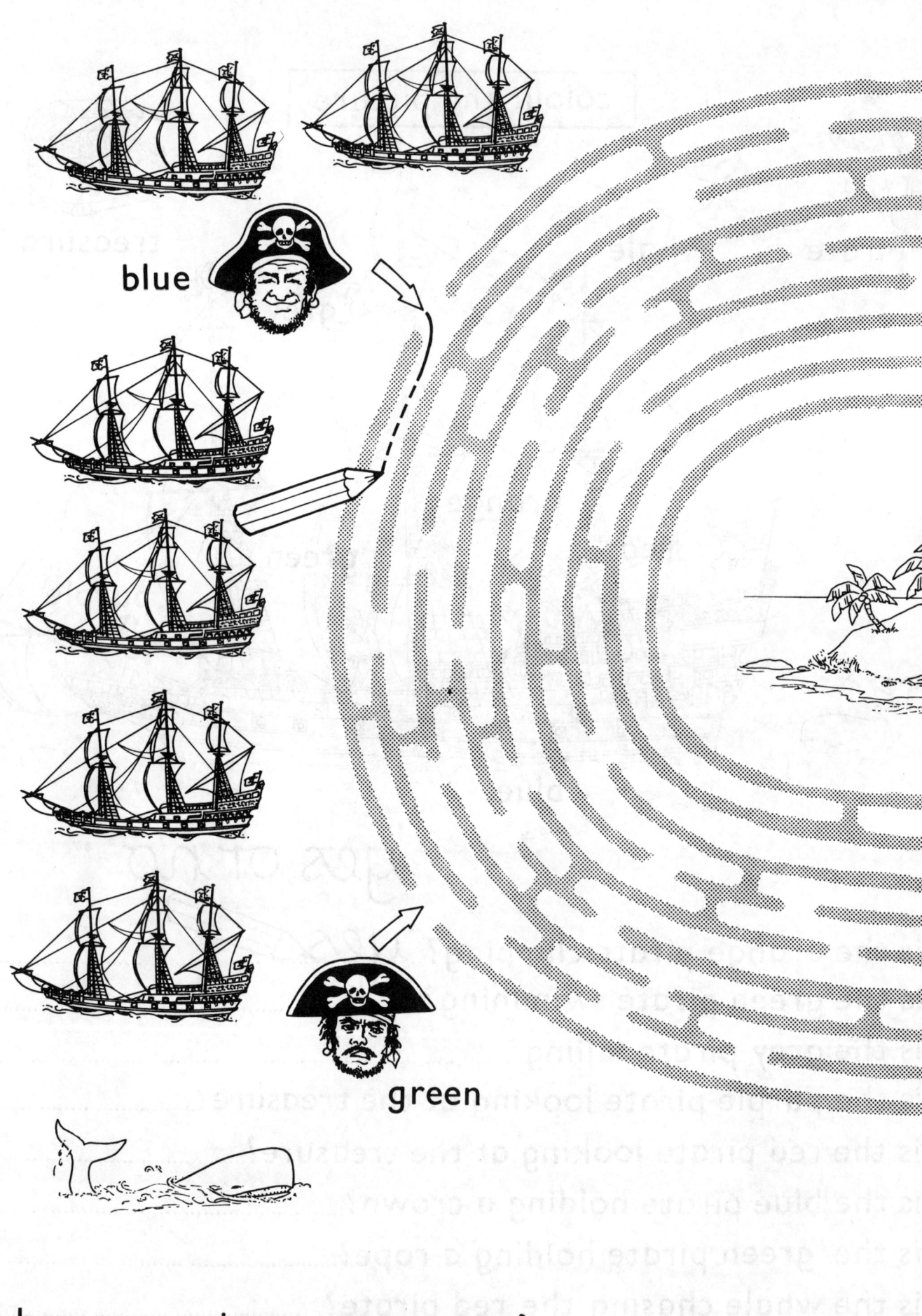

blue

green

how many pirates can you see? ....

how many trees can you see? ....

how many ships can you see? ....

16

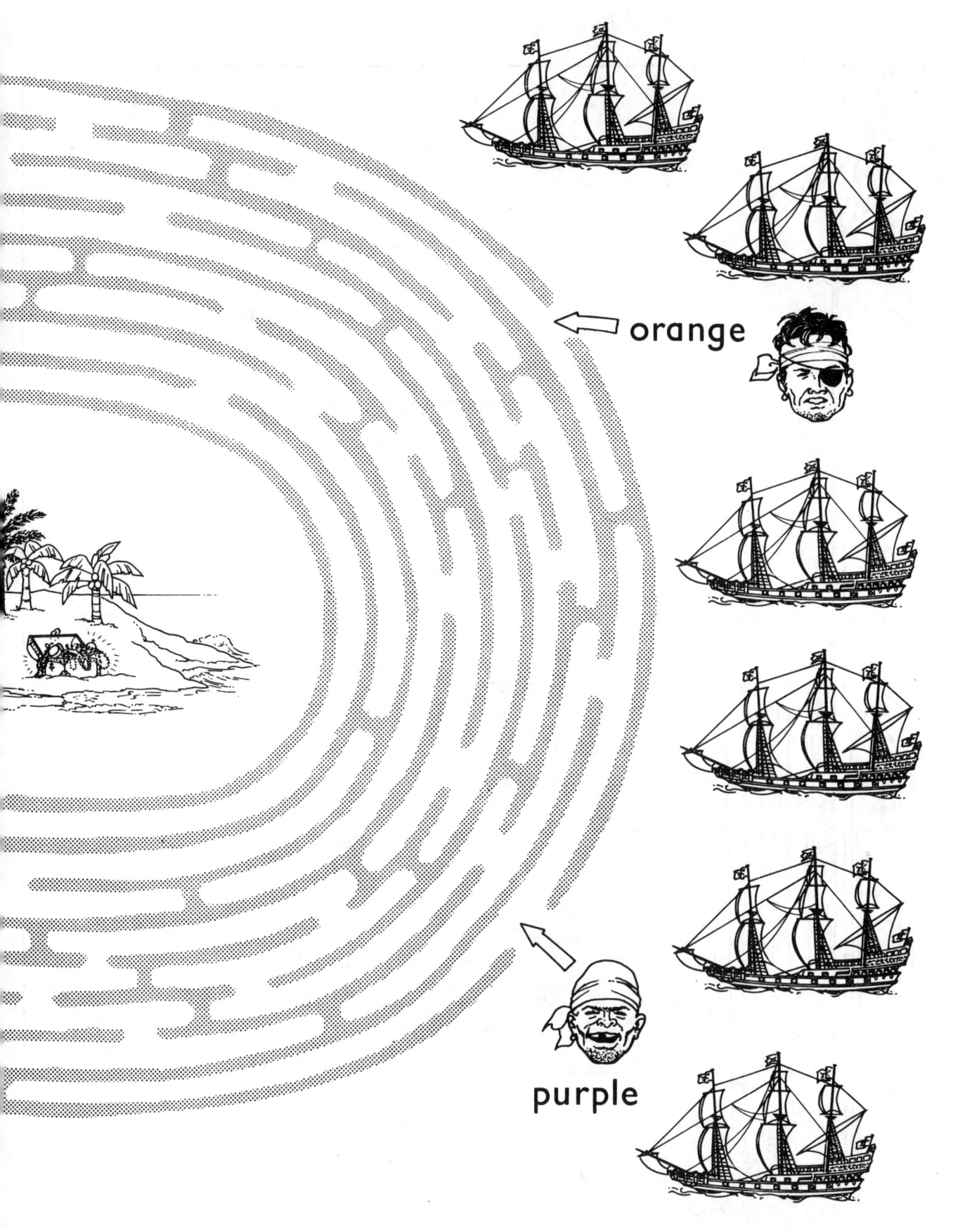

can the blue pirate get to the treasure? ....

can the green pirate get to the treasure? ....

can the orange pirate get to the treasure? ....

can the purple pirate get to the treasure? ....

chain   chair   church   chalk   chopper   chimney

a blue whale	a white shop	a grey church
a red ship	a brown chimney	purple thistles
a black chain	red shoes	pink shells
a brown chair	white chalk	white sheep
a green chopper	orange cheese	a black whistle

the whale is	in the shop
the cheese is	near the sea
the wheel is	near the church
the thistles are	on the roof
the chimney is	near the chair
the chopper is	in the sea
the shells are	by the shop

   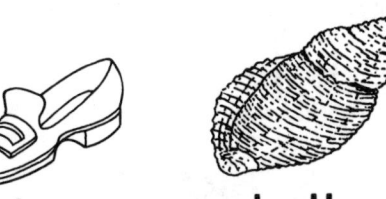

sheep   ship   shop   shoe   shell

whale   wheel   whistle   thistle

wh wh
th th t
sh sh
ch ch c

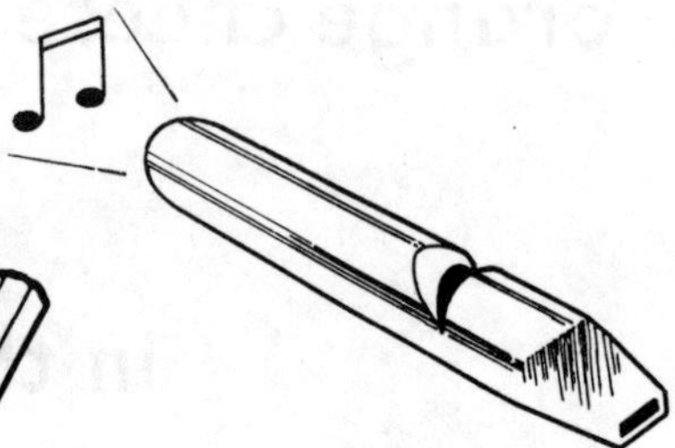

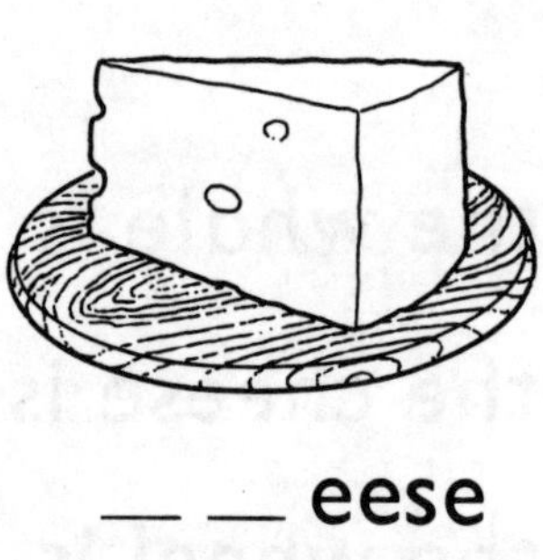

sh oe
__istle
__eese
__ain  
__air
__istle  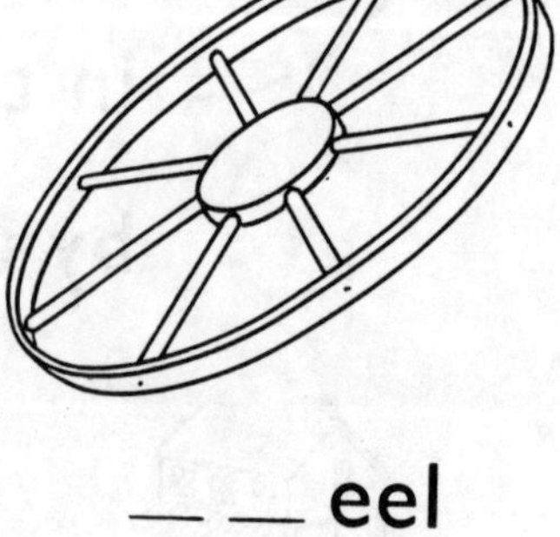 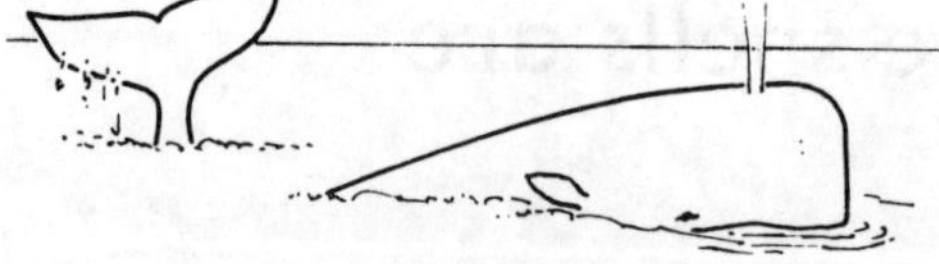
__eel
__ale
__eep 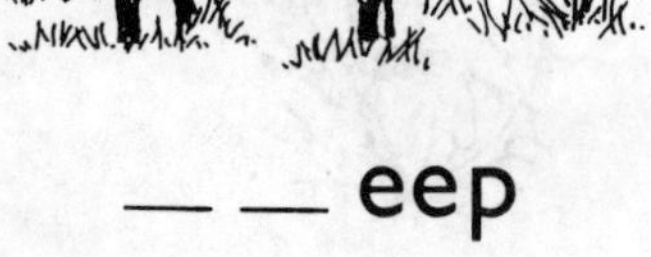  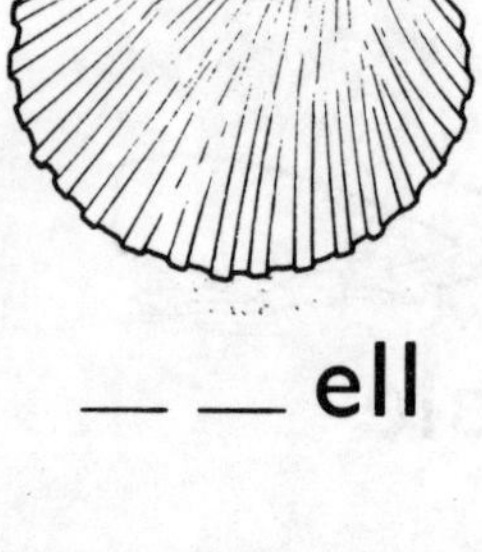
__irteen
__ell

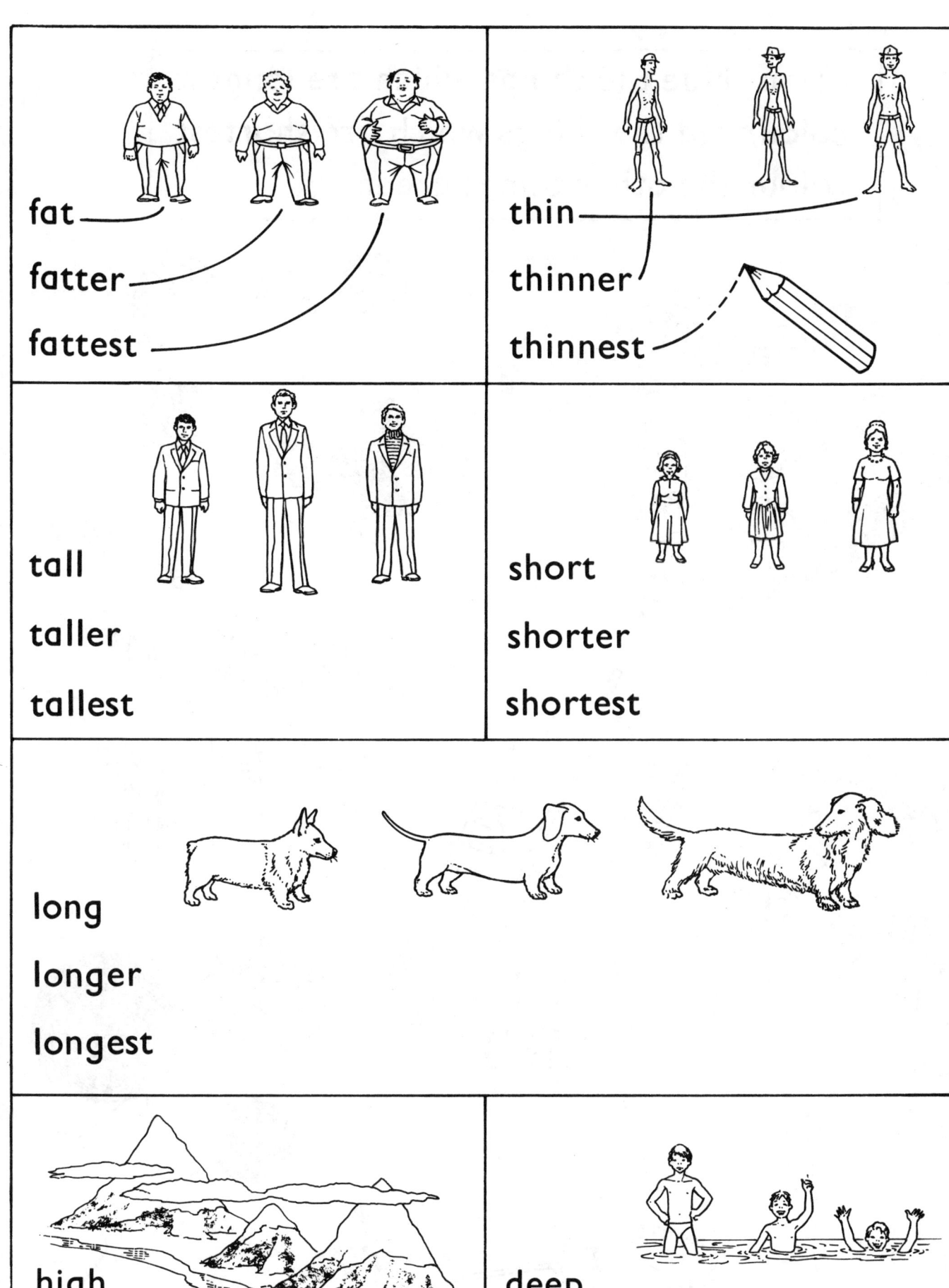

colour blue the things which are longest
colour red the things which are shortest
colour the other things green

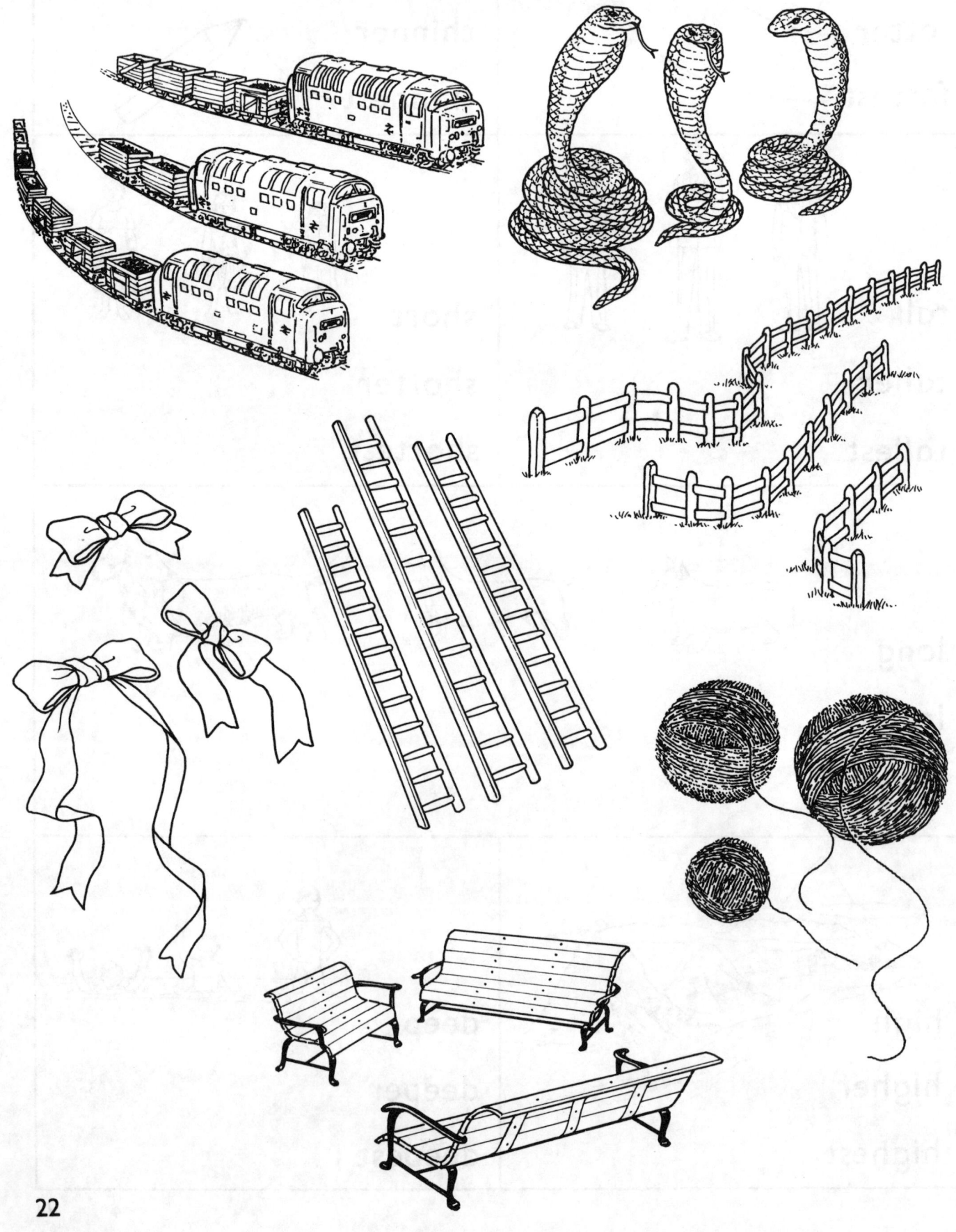

colour orange the animals which are fattest
colour grey the animals which are thinnest
colour the other animals brown

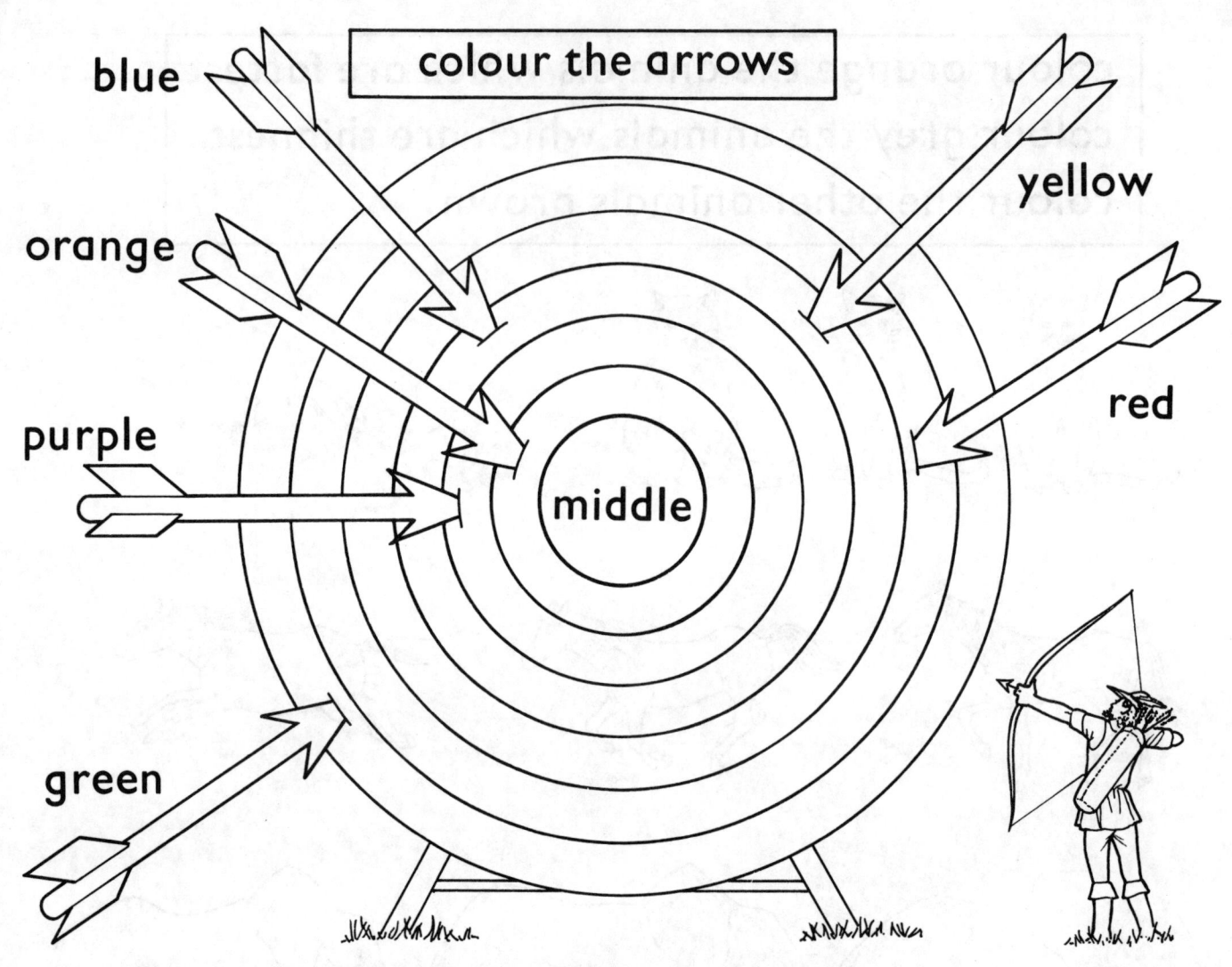

colour the arrows

the orange arrow is **nearer** the middle than the purple arrow

is the blue arrow nearer the middle than the yellow arrow?

is the red arrow nearer the middle than the yellow arrow?

is the purple arrow nearer the middle than the blue arrow?

is the green arrow nearer the middle than the orange arrow?

is the red arrow nearer the middle than the green arrow?

1 2 3 4 5 6 7 8 9 10 11 12 13 14 15

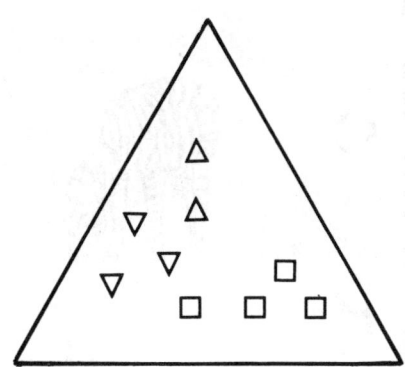
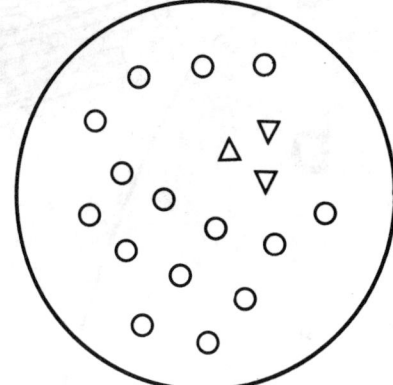
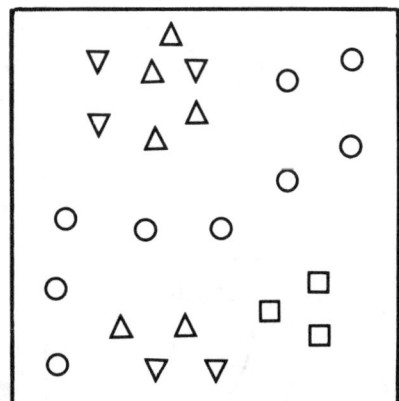

how many little triangles are there in the big triangle?  5

how many little triangles are there in the big square?

how many little circles are there in the big circle?

how many little circles are there in the big square?

how many little squares are there in the big triangle and the big square?

how many little triangles are there in the big triangle and the big circle?

a comes before **b**

apple comes before **ball**

egg comes before | (fish)　　cat　　door |

jam comes before | gate　　hen　　kettle |

leg comes before | ink　　mouse　　jam |

pig comes before | queen　　orange　　nest |

yacht comes before | window　　van　　zebra |

b comes after **a**

ball comes after **apple**

gate comes after | mouse　　fish　　ink |

door comes after | egg　　gate　　cat |

kettle comes after | jam　　mouse　　leg |

tree comes after | rope　　sun　　umbrella |

queen comes after | pig　　van　　yacht |

	stole	steel	(stool)	stoop
	boot	boat	beat	beet
	healing	hearing	seeing	heaping
	soon	stool	soup	spoon
	roof	reef	root	hoof
	shock	clot	clock	check
	well	wood	wheel	wool
	leading	leaping	leaning	learning

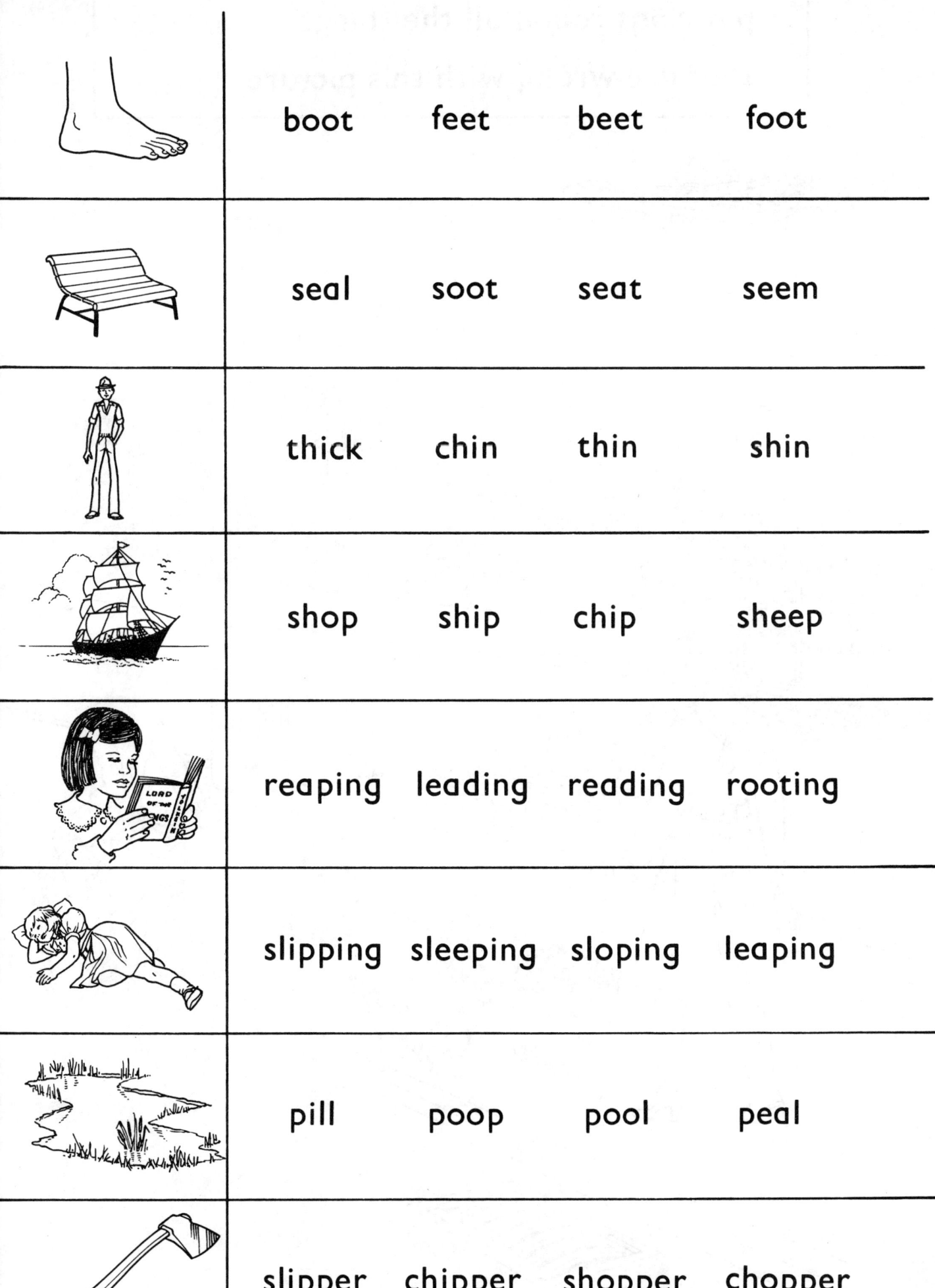

	boot	feet	beet	foot
	seal	soot	seat	seem
	thick	chin	thin	shin
	shop	ship	chip	sheep
	reaping	leading	reading	rooting
	slipping	sleeping	sloping	leaping
	pill	poop	pool	peal
	slipper	chipper	shopper	chopper

put rings round all the things that are wrong with this picture

> how many can you read?

foot	head	ship	church
boot	treasure	sheep	chair
hoof	pirate	shop	chain
roof	seat	shell	chopper
root	seal	shoe	clock

fat	high	hearing	twenty
fatter	higher	seeing	nineteen
fattest	highest	meeting	eighteen
thinner	near	leaping	seventeen
thinnest	nearer	leading	sixteen

two o'clock	eleven o'clock
four o'clock	nine o'clock
six o'clock	seven o'clock
eight o'clock	five o'clock
ten o'clock	three o'clock

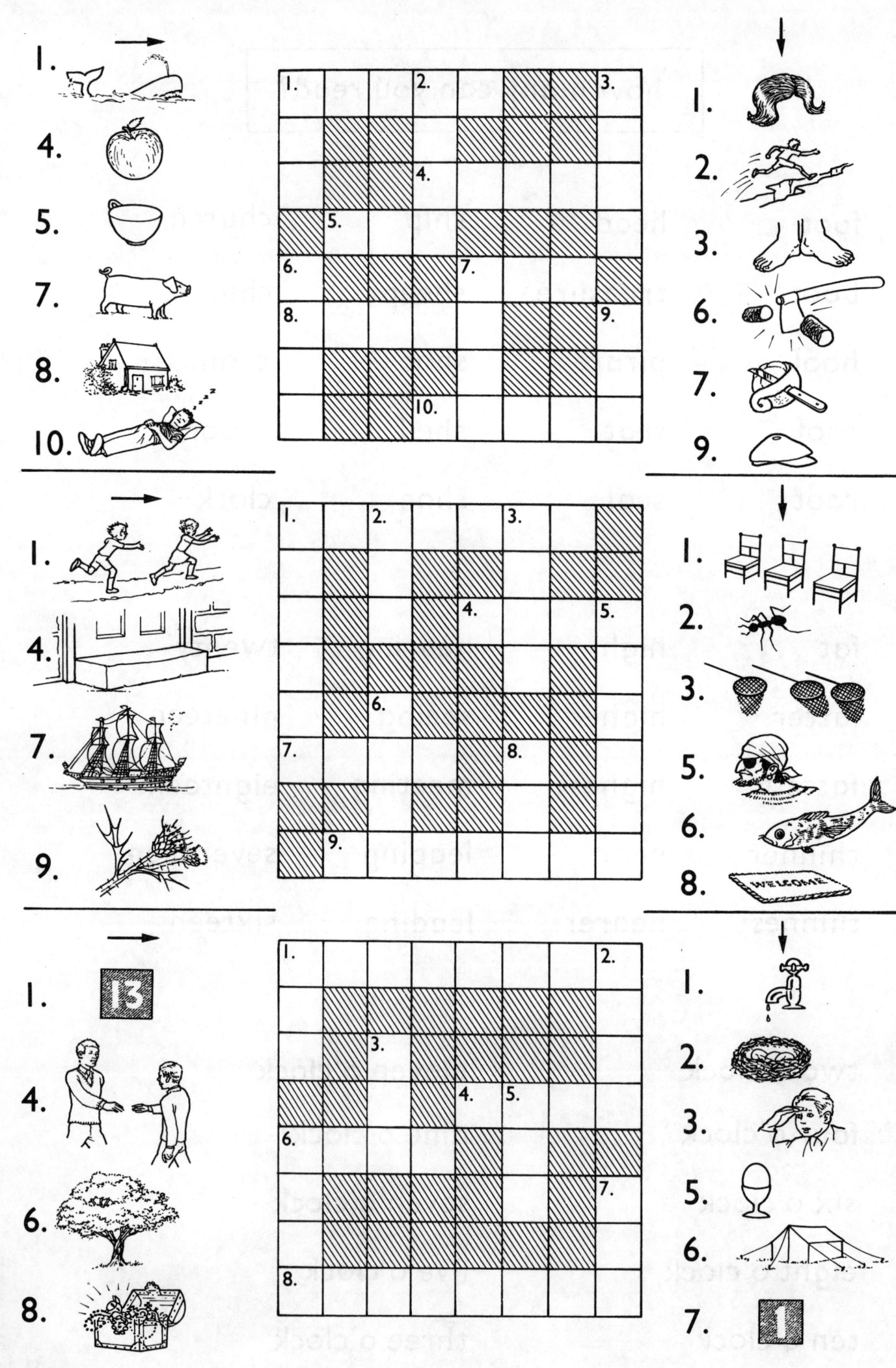